JUMP!

GRASSHOPPERS

Lynette Robbins

PowerKiDS
press
New York

For Fred, who loved the garden and everything in it

Published in 2012 by The Rosen Publishing Group, Inc.
29 East 21st Street, New York, NY 10010

First Edition

Editor: Joanne Randolph
Book Design: Ashley Drago and Erica Clendening

Photo Credits: Cover, p. 10 © Stephen Dalton/age fotostock; p. 4 © www.iStockphoto.com/Jeridu; pp. 5 (right), 9 (right) Hemera/Thinkstock; p. 5 (left) © www.iStockphoto.com/Alexander Shams; p. 6 © www.iStockphoto.com/Mihail Orlov; p. 7 Nigel Dennis/Getty Images; pp. 8, 9 (left), 12–13, 14, 18, 20, 21 Shutterstock.com; p. 11 © www.iStockphoto.com/Will Rennick; p. 15 © www.iStockphoto.com/Ludmila Yilmaz; p. 16 Marten van Dijl/AFP/Getty Images; p. 17 David Maitland/Getty Images; p. 19 Geoff Brightling/Getty Images; p. 22 © www.iStockphoto.com/Manuel Velasco.

Library of Congress Cataloging-in-Publication Data

Robbins, Lynette.
  Grasshoppers / by Lynette Robbins. — 1st ed.
      p. cm. — (Jump!)
  Includes index.
  ISBN 978-1-4488-5015-0 (library binding) — ISBN 978-1-4488-5163-8 (pbk.) — ISBN 978-1-4488-5164-5 (6-pack)
  1. Grasshoppers—Juvenile literature. I. Title.
  QL508.A2R63 2012
  595.7'26—dc22
                                                            2011002786

Manufactured in the United States of America

CPSIA Compliance Information: Batch #WS11PK: For Further Information contact Rosen Publishing, New York, New York at 1-800-237-9932

Contents

Greetings to You, Grasshopper

Have you ever seen a grasshopper? Maybe you have seen one jumping around in your yard or garden. Maybe you have even caught one if you were very quick. Grasshoppers can jump away fast!

Have you ever heard the noise a grasshopper makes? Some kinds of male grasshoppers make a chirping noise by rubbing their wings together. Other kinds of male grasshoppers rub one

As are all insects, grasshoppers are covered by a hard shell called an exoskeleton.

leg against a wing to make the chirping sound.

Grasshoppers are a kind of insect. Like other insects, they have six legs, two **antennae**, and three main body parts. Most kinds of grasshoppers also have two pairs of wings.

Do you see the little points on this grasshopper's back legs? These are called spines. They have a few uses, one of which is to help the grasshopper hold on to plants.

Spines

Here a grasshopper is using its long back legs to jump. A grasshopper's six legs are attached to the middle part of its body, called the thorax.

Grasshoppers Are Everywhere!

Grasshoppers live all over the world, except in places where it is very cold all the time. Grasshoppers like warm weather and places with lots of plants, which they eat. In places where it gets cold in the winter, the grasshoppers die once cold weather comes.

Most grasshoppers live in grassy fields and meadows. Some kinds of grasshoppers live in forests

This grasshopper lives in a grassy field. There are plenty of plants for it to eat there.

or jungles. When people cut down forests to make land for grazing animals or growing crops, they make **habitats** that are just right for grasshoppers. Farmers sometimes think grasshoppers are pests. This is because grasshoppers eat plants. Large numbers of grasshoppers can destroy crops.

It may surprise you, but some grasshoppers live in hot, dry deserts. These grasshoppers may need to fly a long way to find food.

So Many Grasshoppers

There are more than 11,000 different kinds of grasshoppers! All grasshoppers can be divided into two groups based on the size of their antennae. Long-horned grasshoppers have thin antennae that are longer than their bodies. Short-horned grasshoppers have shorter, thicker antennae. Long-horned grasshoppers are also called

Lubber grasshoppers, such as this one, can be different colors depending on where they live. These large grasshoppers have short wings.

LEFT: This is a long-horned grasshopper.

BELOW: Grasshoppers can be quite colorful. This short-horned grasshopper is a nymph, or young grasshopper.

katydids. When some kinds of short-horned grasshoppers travel in huge **swarms**, they are called **locusts**.

Most grasshoppers are about 2 inches (5 cm) long. However, some kinds of lubber grasshoppers are much bigger. They can be 5 inches (13 cm) long! The smallest grasshoppers are pygmy grasshoppers. They are about the size of your thumbnail.

Long-Jumping Grasshoppers

Grasshoppers can walk, fly, or jump. Most of the time, they walk to save energy. However, a grasshopper that needs to get away from a **predator** will jump.

Grasshoppers have strong back legs that help them jump very far. A grasshopper's back legs are about twice as long as its front legs. Most of the time, a grasshopper's back

Grasshoppers have strong muscles in the top part of their back legs. The muscle a grasshopper uses to jump has enough power to lift a bag of sugar.

legs are folded. To jump, the grasshopper straightens its legs and springs into the air. A grasshopper can jump 20 times its own body length. If you could jump as far as a grasshopper, you would be able to hop over two school buses in one bound!

A grasshopper can jump so far because it has a special body part in its knees that works like a spring or rubber band.

Grasshopper Facts

A grasshopper has two large eyes, which are each made up of thousands of tiny eyes. Each of these tiny eyes faces in a different direction. It also has three small eyes on the top of its head. These eyes can see only light and dark.

1

6

Most grasshoppers have two pairs of wings. The front wings are hard. They keep the softer and thinner back wings safe. The back wings are used for flying.

5

After a **nymph molts**, it eats its old **exoskeleton**.

7

Male grasshoppers chirp to draw a mate, or partner, to them and to tell other male grasshoppers to stay away.

Grasshoppers do not have ears on their heads, as people do. However, many kinds of grasshoppers have hearing organs on their knees.

2

Grasshoppers use their antennae as feelers. They also use them to smell. A grasshopper's sense of smell helps it find food.

3

A grasshopper breathes through holes in the sides of its body.

4

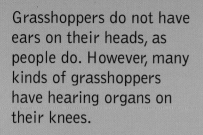

A large group of insects is called a swarm. A swarm of locusts can be so large it can even block out the sun.

8

Some kinds of grasshoppers are helpful to farmers. Instead of eating crops, they eat the weeds that hurt the crops.

9

In some parts of the world, people eat grasshoppers. Sometimes the grasshoppers are dipped in chocolate first.

10

Hungry Hoppers

Grasshoppers spend most of their lives eating. Most grasshoppers are **herbivores**. They eat grasses, shoots, leaves, fruits, and flowers. Some kinds of grasshoppers eat the remains of other animals or hunt and eat small insects.

Grasshoppers have special mouthparts to help them eat. They have two hard, strong jaws called

This grasshopper nymph is eating a caterpillar. Generally only long-horned grasshoppers will eat meat or insects.

mandibles. The mandibles move from side to side, crushing the food between them. On each side of the mandibles, grasshoppers have two fingerlike parts, called palps. The grasshopper uses its palps to bring food into its mouth. A grasshopper's taste buds are in its palps, not in its mouth.

Some grasshoppers will eat only one kind of plant. Others, though, eat whatever plants they find. Can you see the mouthparts that the grasshopper uses to eat here?

Plenty of Predators

A grasshopper is always in danger of becoming another animal's lunch. Many animals eat grasshoppers. Birds, lizards, snakes, rodents, and spiders all dine on grasshoppers. Other larger insects, such as mantises, wasps, and beetles, also eat grasshoppers. Flies often feast on grasshopper eggs.

A lucky grasshopper may escape by jumping away quickly or by flying.

This baby komodo dragon is eating a grasshopper.

Some grasshoppers spit a brown liquid when they are scared. That may **startle** or confuse the predator and give the grasshopper time to get away. Grasshoppers also stay safe by blending in with their surroundings. This is called camouflage. Their green or brown coloring makes them hard to see in a grassy meadow.

This tarantula has caught a grasshopper. It will use its fangs to put poison into the grasshopper to kill it.

Eggs in Hiding

Grasshoppers lay their eggs at the end of summer. A female grasshopper uses a tube on her body called an **ovipositor** to lay her eggs in the soil. She may lay as few as 6 or as many as 150 eggs. The eggs are sausage shaped and smaller than peas. The eggs are covered with foam that comes from the female's body. The foam hardens to keep the eggs safe.

This female grasshopper is laying her eggs under some small stones here.

The eggs stay in the ground through the long, cold winter. When the weather turns warm again in the spring, the eggs are ready to hatch. All the eggs in a nest hole hatch within a few minutes of each other.

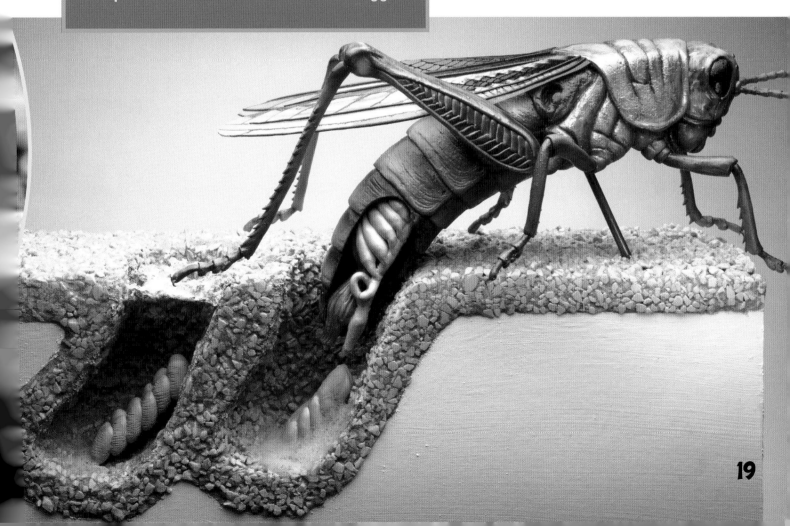

This model shows a grasshopper laying eggs. The hole on the left has a hardened egg casing. On the right, you can see the ovipositor and the foam around the eggs.

Fast-Growing Nymphs

Baby grasshoppers are called nymphs. Nymphs look like tiny adult grasshoppers without wings. After they hatch, nymphs crawl out of the nest hole and start eating.

A nymph grows quickly, but its exoskeleton does not grow. After about five days, the nymph grows too

Here are two grasshopper nymphs on a leaf. Each stage of a grasshopper's life is called an instar.

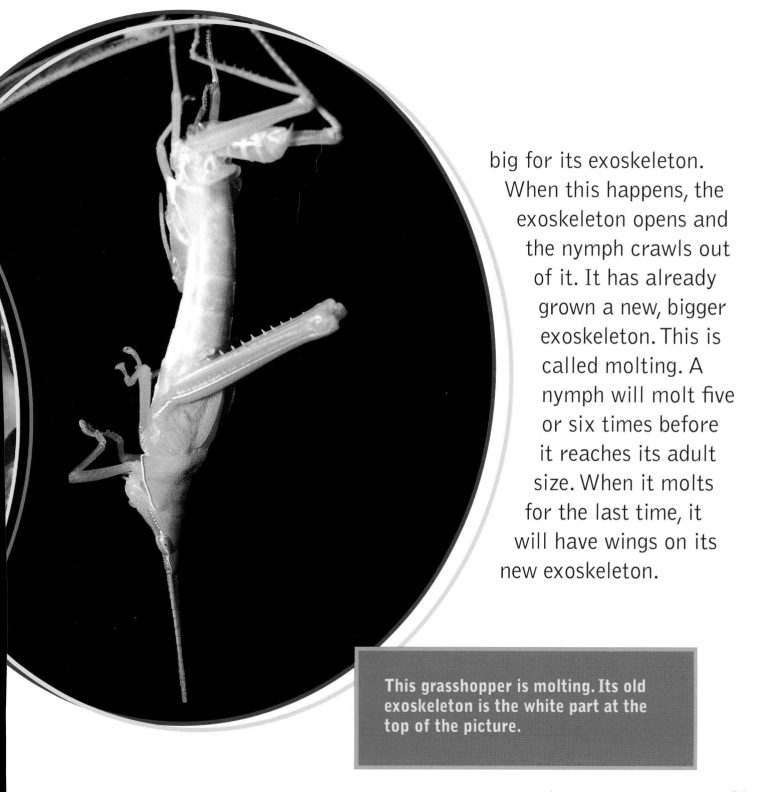

big for its exoskeleton. When this happens, the exoskeleton opens and the nymph crawls out of it. It has already grown a new, bigger exoskeleton. This is called molting. A nymph will molt five or six times before it reaches its adult size. When it molts for the last time, it will have wings on its new exoskeleton.

This grasshopper is molting. Its old exoskeleton is the white part at the top of the picture.

Swarming Locusts

Grasshoppers, with their mighty jumps, are interesting insects. However, when grasshoppers swarm together as locusts, they can destroy a whole crop of wheat in a few hours. What turns these herbivores into such pests?

Sometimes many more short-horned grasshopper eggs are laid than usual. After the eggs hatch, the nymphs run out of food quickly. When they get their wings, millions of adult grasshoppers swarm together. These

Here many locusts are feeding on a plant. Locusts can cause lots of problems for farmers.

locusts fly great distances to find food. Farmers fight swarms by spraying **insecticides**. Most of the time, though, grasshoppers are just hopping insects that are food for many animals.

Glossary

antennae (an-TEH-nee) Thin, rodlike feelers on the heads of certain animals.

exoskeleton (ek-soh-SKEH-leh-tun) The hard covering on the outside of an animal's body that holds and guards the soft insides.

habitats (HA-buh-tats) The kinds of land where animals or plants naturally live.

herbivores (ER-buh-vorz) Animals that eat only plants.

insecticides (in-SEK-tih-sydz) Harmful matter used to kill insects.

locusts (LOH-kusts) Packs of grasshoppers that overrun a place.

mandibles (MAN-dih-bulz) The paired jaws of an insect that generally move side to side.

molts (MOHLTS) Sheds hair, feathers, shell, horns, or skin.

nymph (NIMF) A young insect that has not yet grown into an adult.

ovipositor (oh-vih-PAH-zih-tur) The part of an insect's body that lays eggs.

palps (PALPS) Small, fingerlike parts of an insect's mouth.

predator (PREH-duh-ter) An animal that kills other animals for food.

startle (STAR-tul) To surprise.

swarms (SWORMZ) Large numbers of insects, often moving.

Index

Web Sites

Due to the changing nature of Internet links, PowerKids Press has developed an online list of Web sites related to the subject of this book. This site is updated regularly. Please use this link to access the list:
www.powerkidslinks.com/jump/grasshop/